T0395027

SPORTS SUPERSTARS

CAITLIN CLARK

BY GOLRIZ GOLKAR

BELLWETHER MEDIA·MINNEAPOLIS, MN

TORQUE™

Torque brims with excitement perfect for thrill-seekers of all kinds. Discover daring survival skills, explore uncharted worlds, and marvel at mighty engines and extreme sports. In *Torque* books, anything can happen. Are you ready?

Library of Congress Cataloging-in-Publication Data

LC record for Caitlin Clark available at: https://lccn.loc.gov/2025013833

Editor: Kieran Downs   Designer: Gabriel Hilger

Printed in the United States of America, North Mankato, MN.

TABLE OF CONTENTS

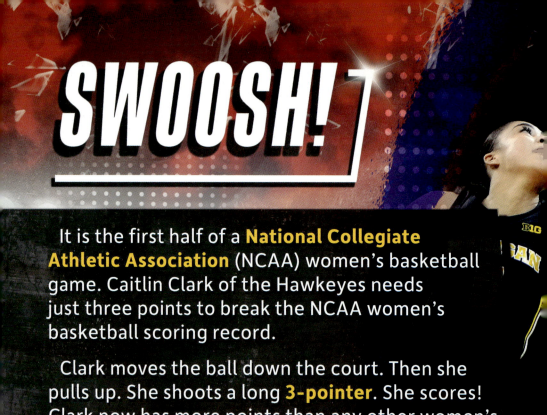

SWOOSH!

It is the first half of a **National Collegiate Athletic Association** (NCAA) women's basketball game. Caitlin Clark of the Hawkeyes needs just three points to break the NCAA women's basketball scoring record.

Clark moves the ball down the court. Then she pulls up. She shoots a long **3-pointer**. She scores! Clark now has more points than any other women's basketball player in NCAA history!

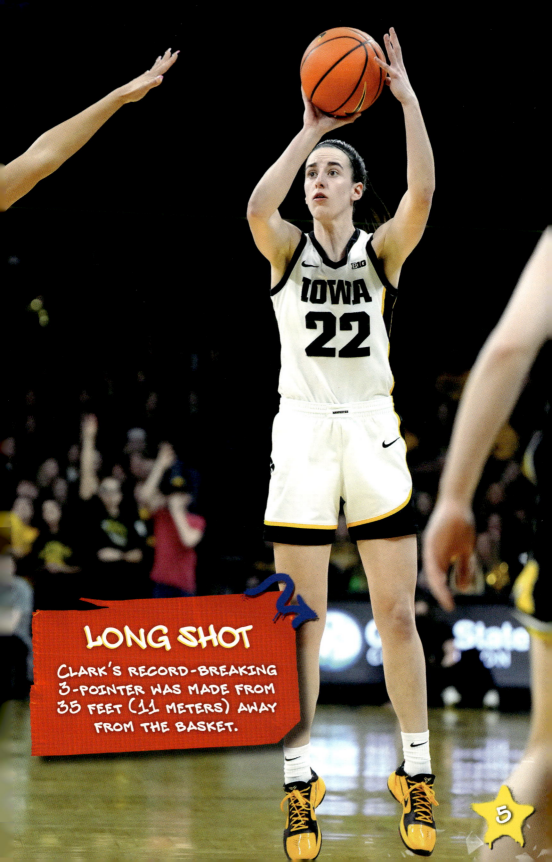

LONG SHOT

CLARK'S RECORD-BREAKING 3-POINTER WAS MADE FROM 35 FEET (11 METERS) AWAY FROM THE BASKET.

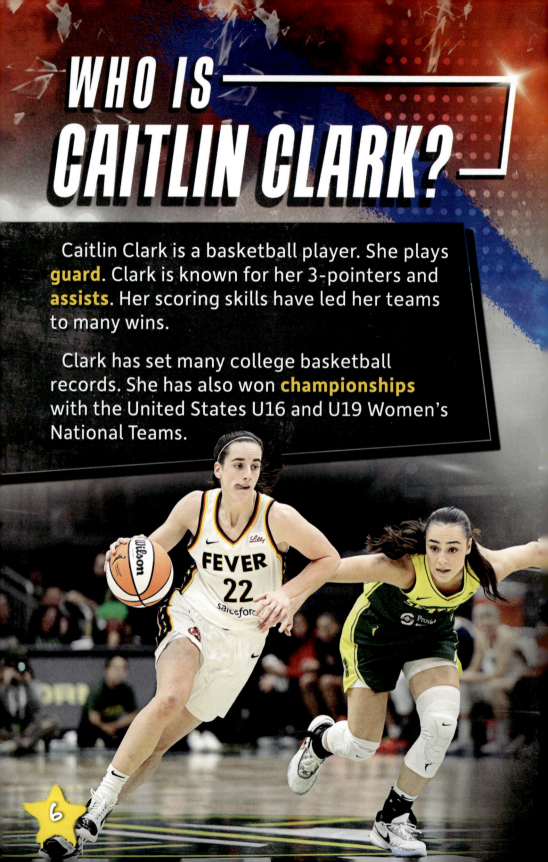

WHO IS CAITLIN CLARK?

Caitlin Clark is a basketball player. She plays **guard**. Clark is known for her 3-pointers and **assists**. Her scoring skills have led her teams to many wins.

Clark has set many college basketball records. She has also won **championships** with the United States U16 and U19 Women's National Teams.

CAITLIN CLARK

BIRTHDAY January 22, 2002

HOMETOWN West Des Moines, Iowa

POSITION guard

HEIGHT 6 feet

DRAFTED Indiana Fever in the first round (1st overall) of the 2024 WNBA Draft

A RISING BASKETBALL STAR

Clark played many sports as a child. She played basketball well by age 5. But there were few opportunities for girls her age. Clark played on boys' teams throughout elementary school. She was a star player.

8

Clark joined the All Iowa Attack youth basketball program starting in sixth grade. She played with them during summers through high school.

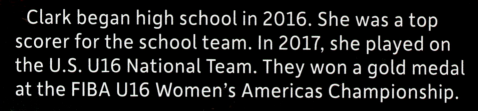

Clark began high school in 2016. She was a top scorer for the school team. In 2017, she played on the U.S. U16 National Team. They won a gold medal at the FIBA U16 Women's Americas Championship.

In 2018, Clark won a national championship with the All Iowa Attack. In 2019, Clark scored 60 points in a single high school game.

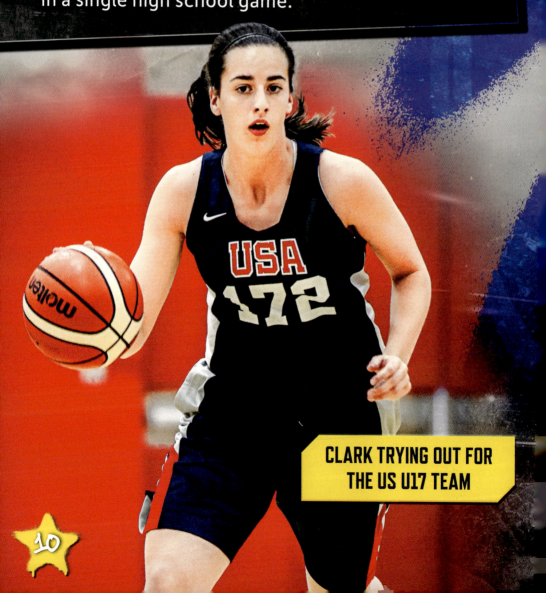

CLARK TRYING OUT FOR THE US U17 TEAM

FAVORITES

ICE CREAM FLAVOR	SPORT BESIDES BASKETBALL	NFL TEAM	MUSICIAN

coffee	golf	Kansas City Chiefs	Luke Combs

In 2019, Clark played on the U.S. U19 Women's National Team. They won a gold medal at the **FIBA U19 Women's Basketball World Cup**. In 2020, she was named Miss Iowa Basketball.

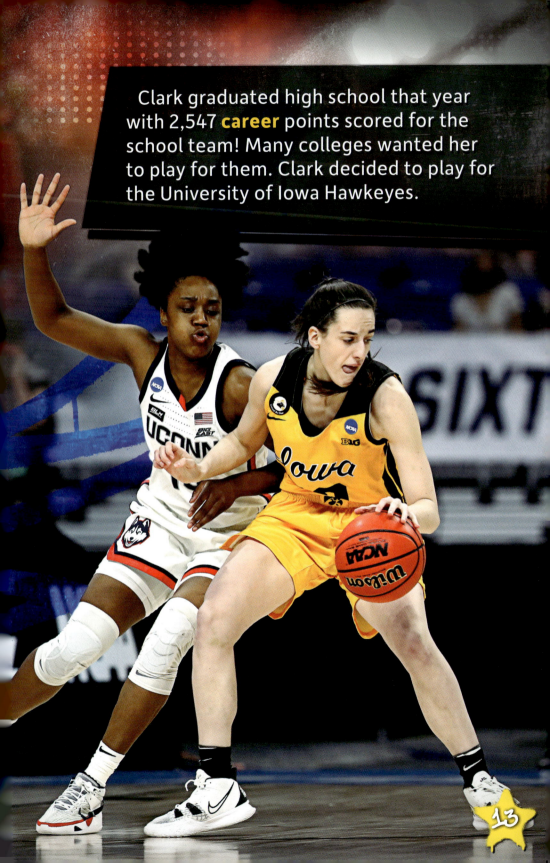

Clark graduated high school that year with 2,547 **career** points scored for the school team! Many colleges wanted her to play for them. Clark decided to play for the University of Iowa Hawkeyes.

13

BREAKING BASKETBALL RECORDS

Clark became one of the top scorers in women's college basketball in her first year. She broke her school's first-year records in total points and assists. She was named the Big 10 **Freshman** of the Year.

Clark also played for the U.S. U19 Women's National Team again in 2021. She helped the team win another World Cup.

CAITLIN CLARK MAP

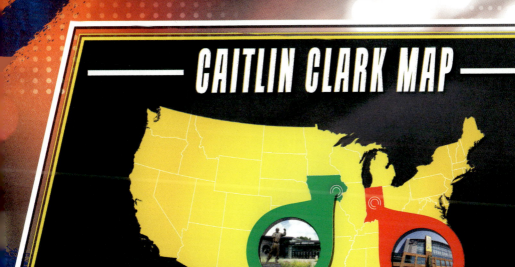

● University of Iowa Hawkeyes,
   Iowa City, Iowa   2020 to 2024

● Indiana Fever,
   Indianapolis, Indiana   2024 to present

Clark was named the Naismith Women's Player of the Year in her third year. She helped Iowa reach the championship of the NCAA **Tournament**. But they lost.

In her final college season, Clark broke the NCAA women's career points record. She broke the overall NCAA points record later that year. Iowa once again reached the championship. But they lost again.

2023 NCAA CHAMPIONSHIP

16

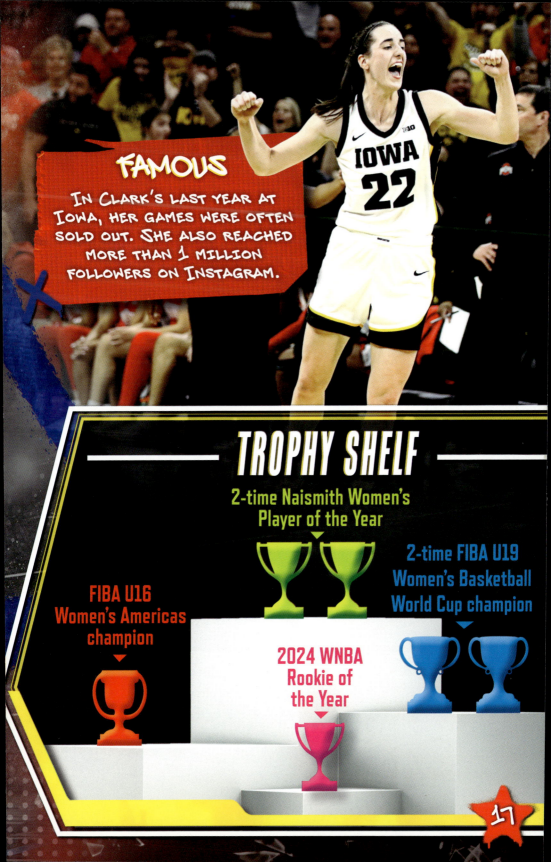

FAMOUS

In Clark's last year at Iowa, her games were often sold out. She also reached more than 1 million followers on Instagram.

TROPHY SHELF

2-time Naismith Women's Player of the Year

2-time FIBA U19 Women's Basketball World Cup champion

FIBA U16 Women's Americas champion

2024 WNBA Rookie of the Year

Clark joined the **Women's National Basketball Association** (WNBA) in 2024. She was **drafted** by the Indiana Fever.

In her first season, Clark set the WNBA record for assists in a season. She was also named the WNBA **Rookie** of the Year. She helped the Fever reach the **playoffs**. But they lost in the First Round.

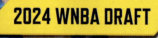

2024 WNBA DRAFT

TIMELINE

— 2017 —

Clark wins a team gold medal at the FIBA U16 Women's Americas Championship

— 2019 —

Clark wins a team gold medal at the FIBA U19 Women's Basketball World Cup

— 2020 —

Clark joins the Hawkeyes

DREAMS COME TRUE

In second grade, Clark wrote that she wanted to play in the WNBA.

— March 2024 —

Clark sets a new NCAA record as the all-time leading scorer in basketball

— April 2024 —

Clark is drafted by the Fever

19

CLARK'S FUTURE

In 2023, Clark started the Caitlin Clark **Foundation**. This group helps young people have a better future. It gives them access to sports, education, and healthy food. It also helps build the communities around them.

HELPING READERS

THE CAITLIN CLARK FOUNDATION SUPPORTS YOUNG READERS. IT HELPED DONATE 22,000 BOOKS TO CHILDREN'S READING PROGRAMS.

Clark hopes to help the Fever win a championship in the future. She is a star on the rise!

21

GLOSSARY

3-pointer—a shot taken from behind a line that counts for three points instead of two

assists—passes to a teammate that result in a score

career—related to the job that a person has for most of their professional life

championships—contests to decide the best team or person

drafted—chosen by a process where professional teams choose high school and college athletes to play for them

FIBA U19 Women's Basketball World Cup—an international basketball tournament between women's basketball teams made of players under the age of 19 held every two years

foundation—an organization that helps people and communities

freshman—a student in their first year of high school or university

guard—a player who is often smaller than other players on the team and is good at ball handling and shooting

National Collegiate Athletic Association—a group in charge of student athletes at colleges in the United States; the National Collegiate Athletics Association is often called the NCAA.

playoffs—games played after the regular season is over; playoff games determine which teams play in the championship game.

rookie—a first-year player in a sports league

tournament—a series of games in which several teams try to win the championship

Women's National Basketball Association—a league for professional basketball in the United States; the Women's National Basketball Association is often called the WNBA.

22

TO LEARN MORE

AT THE LIBRARY

Chandler, Matt. *Caitlin Clark: Basketball Phenom*. North Mankato, Minn.: Capstone Press, 2025.

Hanlon, Luke. *Caitlin Clark: Basketball Star*. Minneapolis, Minn.: ABDO, 2025.

Weiss, Sara. *The Totally Awesome World of Caitlin Clark: Learn All There is to Know About Your Favorite All-Star*. New York, N.Y.: becker&mayer!kids, 2025.

ON THE WEB

FACTSURFER

Factsurfer.com gives you a safe, fun way to find more information.

1. Go to www.factsurfer.com

2. Enter "Caitlin Clark" into the search box and click 🔍.

3. Select your book cover to see a list of related content.

INDEX